The Dirty Joke Book
Volume 1: Pig Laffs

The Dirty Joke Book
Volume 1

Pig Laffs

Compiled by
Kathy and Shelly
www.emailjokes.com

1998
Galde Press, Inc.
Lakeville, Minnesota, U.S.A.

The Dirty Joke Book—Volume 1: Pig Laffs
© Copyright 1998 by Kathy and Shelly
All rights reserved.
Printed in the United States of America.
No part of this book may be used or reproduced in any manner
whatsoever without written permission from the publishers except
in the case of brief quotations embodied in critical articles and reviews.

First Edition
First Printing, 1998

ISBN 1-880090-64-3

Galde Press, Inc.
PO Box 460
Lakeville, Minnesota 55044-0460

Acknowledgement

We would like to thank all those people (and you know who you are) who continually kept us laughing at work. This is a unique collection of side-splitting funny farm jokes, laugh-out-loud one liners that are sure to make you the hit of a party, politically incorrect jokes that can make the straightest stiff crack a smile, and many, many more. We hope that our first collection of jokes, which have orbited the world via e-mail, give you as much pleasure as they have given us. Enjoy!

A Farmer and His Pigs

A farmer buys several pigs, hoping to breed them for ham, bacon, etc. After several weeks, he notices that none of the pigs are getting pregnant and calls a vet for help. The vet tells the farmer that he should try artificial insemination. The farmer doesn't have the slightest idea what this means but, not wanting to display his ignorance, he only asks the vet how he will know when the pigs are pregnant. The vet tells him that they will stop standing around and will instead lie down and wallow in the mud when they are pregnant.

The farmer hangs up and gives this some thought. He comes to the conclusion that artificial insemination means that he has to impregnate the pigs. So, he loads the pigs into his truck, drives them out into the woods, has sex with them all, brings them back and goes to bed.

Next morning, he wakes and looks out at the pigs. Seeing that they are all still standing around, he concludes that the first try didn't take, and loads them in the truck again. He drives them out to the woods, bangs each pig twice for good measure, brings them back and goes to bed.

Next morning, he wakes to find the pigs still just standing around. One more try, he tells himself, and proceeds to load them up and drive them out to the woods. He spends all day shagging the pigs and, upon returning home, falls listlessly into bed.

The next morning, he cannot even raise himself from the bed to look at the pigs. He asks his wife to look out and tell him if the pigs are lying in the mud.

"No," she says, "they're all in the truck and one of them is honking the horn."

Top Fifteen Signs Your Dog Has a Problem with Alcohol

15. Wakes up looking for a little hair o' the human who bit him.
14. Won't go near that darn chuck wagon, but when the bar cart rolls through, he's off like a shot.
13. Lately, you've noticed that he'll even hump a really UGLY leg.
12. No matter what you throw for him to fetch, always returns with a bottle of Cuervo and a lime.
11. Chases pink elephants around the yard instead of squirrels.
10. The only game she'll play with you is "Quarters."
9. Spends more time hugging the toilet bowl than actually slurping from it.
8. Sells house, moves to Vegas, shacks up with beautiful hooker.
7. Justifies quantities consumed by reasoning that they are in "dog beers."
6. When he hikes his leg at the fireplug he keeps falling over backwards.
5. Won't drink out of the toilet unless there's an olive in it.

4. Just signed to do a remake of "Old Yeller" with Kelsey Grammer and Robert Downey, Jr.
3. After a few too many at the office party, tries to pick up the boss's bitch.
2. "Ri *ruv* you, man!!"

And the Number 1 Sign Your Dog Has a Problem With Alcohol...

1. He used to bark—now he just belches the chorus to "Louie, Louie."

A Whale of a Joke

Two whales, a male and a female, are swimming off the coast of Japan when the male whale looks up and sees the whaling ship that killed his father five years ago. Excited at the opportunity to avenge his father's death, the male whale says to the female "Let's go underneath the ship and blow air through our blow holes. That ought to knock their boat over and make them think twice about killing innocent whales." The female whale agrees, and the plan works perfectly.

Once the whaling ship has completely sunk, the male whale notices that most of the sailors are making their way back to the shore by either swimming or in lifeboats. Not willing to let them get away so easily, the male whale yells "They're going to shore! Let's go gobble them up!"

Just then, the female whale becomes less cooperative: *"Hey!"* she says, "I agreed to the blow job, but there is *no way* I'm swallowing seamen!"

A Silly Sparrow

Once upon a time there was a non-conforming sparrow who decided not to fly south for the winter. However, soon the weather turned so cold that he had to reluctantly start winging it south. In a short time, ice began to form on the sparrow's wings, and he fell to the earth in a barnyard, almost frozen to death. A cow passed by and crapped on the little sparrow. The sparrow thought that this was the end of it all.

Suddenly, the manure warmed him and defrosted his wings. Now all warm and happy, he began to sing. A large cat came by and heard the singing, and came over to investigate. The cat cleared away the manure, found the chirping bird and ate him.

Morals of the story:
1. Everyone who shits on you is not necessarily your enemy.
2. Everyone who gets you out of the shit is not necessarily your friend.
3. And, if you are nose-deep in shit, and are feeling warm and happy, keep your mouth shut.

The Tale of Two Cows

Socialism: You have two cows. You keep one and give one to your neighbor.

Communism: You have two cows. The government takes them both and provides you with the milk.

Fascism: You have two cows. The government takes them both and sells you the milk.

Nazism: You have two cows. The government takes them both and shoots you.

Bureaucracy: You have two cows. The government takes them both, shoots one, milks the other, pays you for the milk, then pours it down the drain.

Capitalism: You have two cows. You sell one and buy a bull.

Procterism: You have two cows. You keep them both, force them to produce the milk of four cows, then act surprised when they drop dead.

A Tricky Pet Alligator

A guy walks into a bar with a pet alligator by his side. He puts the alligator up on the bar. He turns to the astonished patrons. "I'll make you a deal. I'll open this alligator's mouth and place my genitals inside. Then the gator will close his mouth for one minute. He'll then open his mouth and I'll remove my unit unscathed. In return for witnessing this spectacle, each of you will buy me a drink."

The crowd murmured their approval. The man stood up on the bar, dropped his trousers, and placed his privates in the alligator's open mouth.

The gator closed his mouth as the crowd gasped.

After a minute, the man grabbed a beer bottle and rapped the alligator hard on the top of its head. The gator opened his mouth and the man removed his genitals—unscathed as promised. The crowd cheered and the first of his free drinks was delivered.

The man stood up again and made another offer. "I'll pay anyone $100 who's willing to give it a try." A hush fell over the crowd. After a while, a hand went up in the back of the bar. A woman timidly spoke up.

"I'll try, but you have to promise not to hit me on the head with the beer bottle."

Why Did the Chicken Cross the Road?

Pat Buchanan: To steal a job from a decent, hard-working American.

Machiavelli: The point is that the chicken crossed the road. Who cares why? The ends of crossing the road justify whatever motive there was.

John Locke: Because he was exercising his natural right to liberty.

Albert Camus: It doesn't matter; the chicken's actions have no meaning except to him.

The Bible: And God came down from the heavens, and He said unto the Chicken, "Thou shalt cross the road." And the Chicken crossed the road, and there was much rejoicing.

Fox Mulder: It was a government conspiracy.

Freud: The fact that you thought that the chicken crossed the road reveals your underlying sexual insecurity.

Darwin: Chickens, over great periods of time, have been naturally selected in such a way that they are now genetically dispositioned to cross roads.

Richard M. Nixon: The chicken did not cross the road. I repeat, the chicken did not cross the road.

Oliver Stone: The question is not "Why did the chicken cross the road?" but is rather "Who was crossing the road at the same time whom we overlooked in our haste to observe the chicken crossing?"

Jerry Seinfeld: Why does anyone cross a road? I mean, why doesn't anyone ever think to ask, "What the heck was this chicken doing walking around all over the place anyway?"

The Pope: That is only for God to know.

Louis Farrakhan: The road, you will see, represents the black man. The chicken crossed the "black man" in order to trample him and keep him down.

Martin Luther King, Jr.: I envision a world where all chickens will be free to cross roads without having their motives called into question.

Immanuel Kant: The chicken, being an autonomous being, chose to cross the road of his own free will.

Grandpa: In my day, we didn't ask why the chicken crossed the road. Someone told us that the chicken had crossed the road, and that was good enough for us.

Dirk Gently (Holistic Detective): I'm not exactly sure why, but right now I've got a horse in my bathroom.

Erich Maria Remarque: The chicken crossed the road because, after his experience with war, he no longer felt at home in his home.

Bill Gates: I have just released the new Chicken 2000, which will both cross roads *and* balance your checkbook, though when it divides 3 by 2 it gets 1.4999999999.

M.C.Escher: That depends on which plane of reality the chicken was on at the time.

George Orwell: Because the government had fooled him into thinking that he was crossing the road of his own free will, when he was really only serving their interests.

Plato: For the greater good.

Karl Marx: It was a historical inevitability.

Nietzsche: Because if you gaze too long across the Road, the Road gazes also across you.

B.F. Skinner: Because the external influences, which had pervaded its sensorium from birth, had caused it to develop in such a fashion that it would tend to cross roads, even while believing these actions to be of its own free will.

Jean-Paul Sartre: In order to act in good faith and be true to itself, the chicken found it necessary to cross the road.

Albert Einstein: Whether the chicken crossed the road or the road crossed the chicken depends upon your frame of reference.

Pyrrho the Skeptic: What road?

The Sphinx: You tell me.

Snoop Doggy Dogg: The bitch saw my 9mm aimed at his muthafuckin' ass.

Buddha: If you ask this question, you deny your own chicken nature.

Emily Dickinson: Because it could not stop for death.

Ralph Waldo Emerson: It didn't cross the road; it transcended it.

Ernest Hemingway: To die. In the rain.

Colonel Sanders: I missed one?

Those Crazy Shepherds

The city-slicker reporter is interviewing an old sheepherder who is tending his flock in the wilds of Wyoming's Big Horn Basin.

"If you don't mind me asking" the reporter says, "what do you do for sex?"

The sheepherder gestures at his flock. "I get all the sex I want."

"You fuck sheep?" the reporter says, aghast. "How can you?"

"Oh, the fucking is easy," the sheepherder says. "The problem is you gotta run around front to kiss 'em."

The Buffalo Theory of Beer Drinking and Brain Development

A herd of buffalo can only move as fast as the slowest buffalo, much like the brain can only operate as fast as the slowest brain cells. The slowest buffalo are the sick and weak, so they die off first, making it possible for the herd to move at a faster pace. Like the buffalo, the weak, slow brain cells are the ones that are killed off by excessive beer drinking and socializing, making the brain operate faster.

The moral of the story: Drink more beer; it will make you smarter.

Is It a Monkey?

A drunk staggers into a fancy restaurant, goes over to a table, and says, "Lady, that' th' ugliesh baby I ever shaw."

"How dare you!" the lady says. She summons the headwaiter and indignantly explains that she has just been insulted.

The headwaiter immediately has the drunk thrown out. "I'm terribly sorry, Madam," the headwaiter says. "This sort of outrage should never occur in a restaurant of our caliber. As a token of apology, allow me to treat you to a complimentary meal."

"That's quite decent of you," the woman says.

The headwaiter peers at the baby and says, "And perhaps the chef can find a banana for your monkey."

A Trick Monkey

A guy walks into a bar with his pet monkey. He orders a drink and while he's drinking it the monkey jumps all around all over the place. The monkey grabs some olives off the bar and eats them, then grabs some sliced limes and eats them, then jumps up on the pool table, grabs the cue ball, sticks it in his mouth and swallows it whole.

The bartender screams at the guy, "Did you see what your monkey just did?"

The guy says, "No, what?"

"He just ate the cue ball off my pool table, whole!" says the bartender.

"Yeah, that doesn't surprise me," replied the patron, "he eats everything in sight, the little bastard. I'll pay for the cue ball and stuff."

He finishes his drink, pays his bill, and leaves.

Two weeks later he's in the bar again, and he has his monkey with him.

He orders a drink and the monkey starts running around the bar again. While the man is drinking his drink, the monkey finds a maraschino cherry on the bar. He grabs it, sticks it up his butt, pulls it out, and eats it.

The bartender is disgusted. "Did you see what your monkey did now?" he asks.

"Now what?" responds the patron.

"Well, he stuck a maraschino cherry up his butt, then pulled it out and ate it!" says the barkeeper.

"Yeah, that doesn't surprise me," replied the patron. "He still eats everything in sight, but ever since he ate that damn cue ball, he measures everything first!"

True Story

Bob Tucker wakes up one morning to find a gorilla in his tree. He looks through the phone book for the most affordable and reputable gorilla removal service and calls the number.

"Is it a boy or girl gorilla?" the service man asks.

"Boy," Bob says.

"Oh yeah, I can do it. I'll be right there."

An hour later the service man shows up with a stick, a chihuahua, a shotgun, and a pair of handcuffs. He then gives the guy some instructions.

"Now, I'm going to climb this tree and poke the gorilla with the stick until he falls. When he does, the trained chihuahua will bite the gorilla's testicles off. The gorilla will then cross his hands to protect himself and allow you to put the handcuffs on."

"What do I do with the shotgun?" Bob asks.

"If I fall out of the tree before the gorilla, shoot the dog."

Mighty Mice

Three mice were sitting at a bar talking about how tough they were. The first mouse slams a shot and says, "I play with mouse traps for fun. I'll run into one on purpose and as it is closing on me, I grab the bar and bench press it twenty or thirty times." And, with that, he slams another shot. The second mouse slams a shot and says, "That's nothing. I take those deacon tablets, cut them up, and snort them, just for the fun of it." And, with that, he slams another shot.

The third mouse slams a shot, gets up, and walks away. The first two mice look at each other, then turn to the third mouse and ask, "Where the hell are you going?"

The third mouse stops and replies, "I'm going home to fuck the cat."

The Bonuses of a Seeing-Eye Dog

A blind woman walks into a department store, grabs her seeing-eye dog by the tail, and starts swinging him around over her head.

"May I help you?" the clerk inquires.

"No thank you," the blind woman says. "I'm just taking a look around!"

Horsing Around

A horse and a rabbit are playing in a meadow. The horse falls into a mudhole and is sinking. He calls to the rabbit to go and get the farmer to help pull him out to safety. The rabbit runs to the farm but the farmer can't be found.

He drives the farmer's Mercedes back to the mudhole and ties some rope around the bumper. He then throws the other end of the rope to his friend, the horse, and drives the car forward, saving him from sinking!

A few days later, the rabbit and horse were playing in the meadow again and this time, the rabbit falls into the mudhole. The rabbit yells to the horse to go and get some help from the farmer. The horse said, "I think I can stand over the hole!" So he stretched over the width of the hole and said, "Grab for my 'thingy' and pull yourself up." And the rabbit did and pulled himself to safety.

The moral of the story: If you are hung like a horse, you don't need a Mercedes.

The Cowboy and Indian

A ventriloquist cowboy walks into town and sees an Indian sitting near his pad.
Cowboy: Hey, cool dog! Mind if I speak to him?
Indian: Dog no talk.
Cowboy: Hey dog, how's it going?
Dog: Doin' all right.
Indian: (extreme look of shock)
Cowboy (pointing at Indian): Is this your owner?
Dog: Yep.
Cowboy: How's he treat you?
Dog: Real good. He walks me twice a day, feeds me great food, and takes me to the lake once a week to play.
Indian: (look of disbelief)

Cowboy: Mind if I talk to your horse?

Indian: Horse no talk.

Cowboy: Hey horse, how's it going?

Horse: Cool!

Indian: (more extreme look of shock)

Cowboy (pointing at Indian): Is this your owner?

Horse: Yep.

Cowboy: How's he treat you?

Horse: Pretty good, thanks for asking. He rides me regularly, brushes me down often, and keeps me in the barn to protect me from the elements.

Indian: (total look of amazement)

Cowboy: Mind if I talk to your sheep?

Indian: Sheep lie!!

Penguin Pinball

A Mexican newspaper reports that bored Royal Air Force pilots stationed on the Falkland Islands have devised what they consider a marvelous new game. Noting that the local penguins are fascinated by airplanes, the pilots search out a beach where the birds are gathered and fly slowly along it at the water's edge. Perhaps ten thousand penguins turn their heads in unison watching the planes go by, and when the pilots turn around and fly back, the birds turn their heads in the opposite direction, like spectators at a slow-motion tennis match. Then, the paper reports, "The pilots fly out to sea and directly to the penguin colony and overfly it. Heads go up, up, up, and ten thousand penguins fall over gently onto their backs."

A Comparison Between Dogs And Men

Why Dogs Are Better Than Men

Dogs do not have problems expressing affection in public.

Dogs miss you when you're gone.

You never wonder whether your dog is good enough for you.

Dogs feel guilt when they've done something wrong.

Dogs don't brag about whom they have slept with.

Dogs don't criticize your friends.

Dogs admit when they're jealous.

Dogs do not play games with you—except fetch (and then never laugh at how you throw).

Dogs are happy with any video you choose to rent, because they know the most important thing is that you're together.

Dogs don't feel threatened by your intelligence.

You can train a dog.

Dogs are already in touch with their inner puppies.

You are never suspicious of your dog's dreams.

Gorgeous dogs don't know they're gorgeous.

The worst social disease you can get from dogs is fleas. (Okay, the *really* worst disease you can get from them is rabies, but there's a vaccine for it, and you get to kill the one that gives it to you.)

Dogs understand what "no" means.

Dogs don't need therapy to undo their bad socialization.

Dogs don't make a practice of killing their own species.

Dogs understand if some of their friends cannot come inside.

Dogs think you are a culinary genius.

You can house train a dog.

You can force a dog to take a bath.

Dogs don't correct your stories.

Middle-aged dogs don't feel the need to abandon you for a younger owner.
Dogs aren't threatened by a woman with short hair.
Dogs aren't threatened by two women with short hair.
Dogs don't mind if you do all the driving.
Dogs don't step on the imaginary brake.
Dogs admit it when they're lost.
Dogs don't weigh down your purse with their stuff.
Dogs do not care whether you shave your legs.
Dogs take care of their own needs.
Dogs aren't threatened if you earn more than they do.
Dogs mean it when they kiss you.
Dogs are nice to your relatives.

How Dogs and Men Are the Same

Both take up too much space on the bed.
Both have irrational fears about vacuum cleaning.
Both are threatened by their own kind.
Both like to chew wood.
Both mark their territory.
Both are bad at asking you questions.
Neither tells you what's bothering them.
Both tend to smell riper with age.
The smaller ones tend to be more nervous.
Both have an inordinate fascination with women's crotches.
Neither does any dishes.
Both fart shamelessly.
Neither of them notice when you get your hair cut.
Both like dominance games.

Both are suspicious of the postman.

Neither knows how to talk on the telephone.

Neither understands what you see in cats.

Why Men Are Better Than Dogs

Men only have two feet to track in mud.

Men can buy you presents.

Men don't have to play with every man they see when you take them around the block.

Men are a little bit more subtle.

Men don't eat cat turds on the sly.

Men open their own cans.

Dogs have dog breath all the time.

Men can do math stuff.

Holiday Inns accept men.

Layoffs—Press Release

The recent announcement that Donner and Blitzen have elected to take the early reindeer retirement package has triggered a good deal of concern about whether they will be replaced, and about other restructuring decisions at the North Pole.

Streamlining was appropriate in view of the reality that the North Pole no longer dominates the season's gift distribution business. Home shopping channels and mail order catalogs have diminished Santa's market share and he could not sit idly by and permit further erosion of the profit picture. The reindeer downsizing was made possible through the purchase of a late model Japanese sled for the CEO's annual trip. Improved productivity from Dasher and Dancer, who summered at the Fuqua School of Business, is anticipated and should take up the slack with no discernible loss of service. Reduction in reindeer will also lessen airborne environmental emissions for which the North Pole has been cited and received unfavorable press.

I am pleased to inform you and yours that Rudolph's role will not be disturbed. Tradition still counts for something at the North Pole. Management denies, in the strongest possible language, the earlier leak that Rudolph's nose got that way not from the cold, but from substance abuse. Calling Rudolph "a lush who was into the sauce and never did pull his share of the load" was an unfortunate comment, made by one of Santa's helpers and taken out of context at a time of year when he is known to be under executive stress.

As a further restructuring, today's global challenges require the North Pole to continue to look for better, more competitive steps. Effective immediately, the following economy measures are to take place in the "Twelve Days of Christmas" subsidiary:

The partridge will be retained, but the pear tree never turned out to be the cash crop forecasted. It will be replaced by a plastic hanging plant, providing considerable savings in maintenance.

The two turtle doves represent a redundancy that is simply not cost effective. In addition, their romance during working hours could not be condoned. The positions are therefore eliminated.

The three French hens will remain intact. After all, everyone loves the French.

The four calling birds were replaced by an automated voice mail system, with a call waiting option. An analysis is under way to determine who the birds have been calling, how often and how long they talked.

The five golden rings have been put on hold by the Board of Directors. Maintaining a portfolio based on one commodity could have negative implications for institutional investors. Diversification into other precious metals as well as a mix of T-bills and high-technology stocks appear to be in order.

The six geese-a-laying constitute a luxury which can no longer be afforded. It has long been felt that the production rate of one egg per goose per day is an example of the decline in productivity. Three geese will be let go, and an upgrading in the selection procedure by personnel will assure management that from now on every goose it gets will be a good one.

The seven swans-a-swimming is obviously a number chosen in better times. The function is primarily decorative. Mechanical swans are on order. The current swans will be retrained to learn some new strokes and therefore enhance their outplacement.

As you know, the eight maids-a-milking concept has been under heavy scrutiny by the EEOC. A male/female balance in the work force is being sought. The more militant maids consider this a dead-end job with no upward mobility. Automation of the process may permit the maids to try a-mending, a-mentoring, or a-mulching.

Nine ladies dancing has always been an odd number. This function will be phased out as these individuals grow older and can no longer do the steps.

Ten lords-a-leaping is overkill. The high cost of lords plus the expense of international air travel prompted the Compensation Committee to suggest replacing this group with ten out-of-work congressmen. While leaping ability may be somewhat sacrificed, the savings are significant because we expect an oversupply of unemployed congressmen this year.

Eleven pipers piping and twelve drummers drumming is a simple case of the band getting too big. A substitution with a string quartet, a cutback on new music, and no uniforms will produce savings which will drop right down to the bottom line. We can expect a substantial reduction in assorted people, fowl, animals, and other expenses. Though incomplete, studies indicate that stretching deliveries over twelve days is inefficient. If we can drop ship in one day, service levels will be improved. Regarding the lawsuit filed by the attorney's association seeking expansion to include the legal profession ("thirteen lawyers-a-suing"), action is pending.

Lastly, it is not beyond consideration that deeper cuts may be necessary in the future to stay competitive. Should that happen, the Board will request management to scrutinize the Snow White Division to see if seven dwarfs is the right number.

A Kitty Joke

Little Lucy went out into the garden and saw her cat Tiddles lying on the ground with its eyes shut and its legs in the air.

She called her dad and on seeing the cat he said, "I'm afraid Tiddles is dead, Lucy."

"But Daddy, why are his legs sticking up in the air like that ?"

At a loss for something to say, the father replied, "Tiddles' legs are pointing straight up in the air so that it will be easier for God to float down from heaven above and grab a leg and lift Tiddles up to heaven."

Little Lucy seemed to take Tiddles' death quite well. However two days later when her father came home from work Lucy had tears in her eyes and said: "Mommy almost died this morning."

Fearing something terrible had happened, the father shook the girl and shouted, "What do you mean, Lucy? Tell Daddy!"

"Well, soon after you left for work this morning, I saw Mommy lying on the floor with her legs in the air, and she was shouting, 'Oh God! I'm coming, I'm coming!' and if it hadn't been for the milkman holding her down, she would definitely have gone, Daddy."

The Chicken

An old farmer decided it was time to get a new rooster for his hens. The current rooster was still doing an okay job, but he was getting on in years. And the farmer figured getting a new rooster couldn't hurt anything. So he buys a young cock from the local rooster emporium and turns him loose in the barnyard.

Well, the old rooster sees the young one strutting around and he gets a little worried. So, they're trying to replace me, thinks the old rooster. I've got to do something about this. He walks up to the new bird and says,

"So you're the new stud in town? I bet you really think you're hot stuff, don't you? Well I'm not ready for the chopping block yet. I'll bet I'm still the better bird. And to prove it, I challenge you to a race around that hen house over there. We'll run around it ten times and whoever finishes first gets to have all the hens for himself."

Well, the young rooster was a proud sort, and he definitely thought he was more than a match for the old guy. "You're on," said the young rooster.

"And since I know I'm so great, I'll even give you a head start of half a lap. I'll still win easy," said the young rooster.

So the two roosters go over to the hen house to start the race with all the hens gathering around to watch. The race begins and all the hens start cheering the roosters on. After the first lap, the old rooster is still maintaining his lead. After the second lap, the old guy's lead has slipped a little but he's still hanging in there. Unfortunately the old rooster's lead continues to slip each time around, and by the fifth lap he's just barely in front of the young rooster.

By now the farmer has heard all the commotion. He runs into the house, gets his shotgun, and runs out to the barnyard figuring a fox or something is after his chickens. When he gets there, he sees the two roosters running around the hen house, with the old rooster still slightly in the lead. He immediately takes his shotgun, aims, fires, and blows the young rooster away.

As he walks away slowly, he says to himself—

"Damn, that's the third gay rooster I've bought this month."

The Ant and the Grasshopper

The Original Version:

The Ant busts his butt in the withering summer heat, building his house and laying up supplies for the winter. The Grasshopper thinks him a fool and laughs, dances, and plays the summer away. Come winter, the Ant is warm and well fed. The Grasshopper has no food or shelter and dies out in the cold. The End.

The New (Liberal) Version:

The Ant busts his butt in the withering summer heat, building his house and laying up supplies for the winter. The Grasshopper thinks him a fool and laughs, dances, and plays the summer away. Come winter, the shivering Grasshopper calls a press conference and demands to know why the Ant can be warm and well fed while others are cold and starving.

CBS, NBC, ABC, and CNN contrast pictures of the shivering Grasshopper with pictures of the Ant in his meager but comfortable home with a table full of food. America is stunned by the sharp contrast! How can it be, in a country of such wealth, that the poor Grasshopper is allowed to suffer so?

Then a representative of the NAAGB (the National Association for the Advancement of Green Bugs) shows up on "Night Line" and charges the Ant with Green Bias, making the case that the Grasshopper is the victim of years of greenish. Kermit the Frog appears on Oprah, with the Grasshopper, making everybody cry when he sings "It's Not Easy Being Green." Bill and Hillary Clinton make a special appearance on the "CBS Evening News." They tell a concerned Dan Rather they will do everything they can for the Grasshopper, who has been denied the prosperity he deserves by those who benefited unfairly during the summer (or, as Bill refers to it, the temperature of the 80s)

Finally, the EEOC drafts the Economic Equity and Anti-Greenism Act, retroactive to the beginning of the summer. The Ant is fined for failing to hire a proportionate number of green bugs. Moreover, having nothing left to pay his retroactive taxes, the Government confiscates his home and possessions. The story ends with the Grasshopper eating the last of the Ant's food while the Government house he is in (which looks a lot like the Ant's house) crumbles around him since he doesn't bother to maintain it. The Ant has disappeared in the snow. On the TV, which the Grasshopper bought using Welfare and SSI proceeds, Bill Clinton is standing before a wildly applauding group of Democrats announcing that a New Era of Fairness has dawned in America.

Parrot or Person?

An older gentleman was standing at a bus stop, observing a young man with orange, green, and blue spiked hair. After a few moments, the young man said, "What's the matter, old man, haven't you ever done anything wild?"

The old man smiled and said, "Well, yes. I once had sex with a parrot, and I was wondering if you might be my son…"

The Mule and the Mother-in-Law

A newlywed farmer and his wife were visited by her mother, who immediately demanded an inspection of the place. While they were walking through the barn, the farmer's mule suddenly reared up and kicked the mother-in-law in the head, killing her instantly.

At the funeral service a few days later, the farmer stood near the casket and greeted folks as they walked by. The pastor noticed that whenever a woman would whisper something to the farmer, he would nod his head yes and say something. Whenever a man walked by and whispered to the farmer, he would shake his head no and mumble a reply.

Curious, the pastor later asked the farmer what that was all about. The farmer replied, "The women would say, 'What a terrible tragedy,' and I would nod my head and say, 'Yes, it was.' The men would ask, 'You wanna sell that mule?' and I would shake my head and say, 'Can't. It's all booked up for a year.'"

The Talking Horse

A traveling salesman stopped alongside a field on a country road to rest a few minutes. The man had just closed his eyes when a horse came to the fence and began to boast about his past. "Yes sir, I'm a fine horse. I've run in twenty-five races and won over five million dollars. I keep my trophies in the barn."

The salesman computed the value of having a talking horse, found the horse's owner, and offered a handsome sum for the animal.

"Aw, you don't want that horse," said the farmer.

"Yes I do," said the salesman, "and I'll give you one hundred thousand dollars for the horse."

Recognizing a good deal, the farmer said without hesitation, "He's yours."

While he wrote out his check, the salesman asked, "By the way, why wouldn't I want your horse?"

"Because," said the farmer, "he's a liar—he never won a race in his life."

Noah's Ark

When Noah took the animals on the Ark, in order to keep a stable population he issued each of the males a claim check and made them leave their privates at the door.

On the night before they landed, the male monkey eased over to the female monkey and whispered "There's gonna be hot times tomorrow, baby. I stole the elephant's ticket stub!"

The Penguin with Car Trouble

This penguin is driving his new car through the barren, arid Arizona desert. He is an Antarctic penguin, so he has the air conditioning on "max."

Suddenly he hears a loud "bang" from under the hood. The air blowing from the louvers quickly turns hot. So the penguin pulls to the side of the dirt road and looks under the hood.

Since he's a penguin, he doesn't know much about mechanics, so he decides to head to the nearest garage. Fortunately, there's a small town just a few miles down the road. He pulls into the garage and turns the car over to the mechanic, who tells him to walk around town for a few minutes and come back.

The penguin waddles slowly around town, trying to stay in the shadows. He feels himself getting overheated when he sees an ice cream parlor. He goes in and orders a large vanilla cone.

Of course, it's difficult for him to eat a cone with his beak, so he gets a lot of ice cream on his face and "tux" front. He sees the mechanic motioning to him from across the street, so he hurries out without cleaning off the ice cream.

As he comes into the garage, the mechanic says, "Looks like you blew a seal."

The penguin answers, "No, it's just ice cream."

The Statues

For decades, two heroic statues, one male and one female, faced each other in a city park, until one day an angel came down from heaven.

"You've been such exemplary statues," he announced to them, "that I'm going to give you a special gift. I'm going to bring you both to life for thirty minutes, in which you can do anything you want."

And with a clap of his hands, the angel brought the statues to life. The two approached each other a bit shyly, but soon dashed for the bushes, from which shortly emerged a good deal of giggling, laughter, and shaking of branches.

Fifteen minutes later, the two statues emerged from the bushes, wide grins on their faces.

"You still have fifteen more minutes," said the angel, winking at them.

Grinning even more widely, the female statue turned to the male statue and said, "Great! Only this time you hold the pigeon down and I'll crap on it's head!"

The Snake and the Rabbit

A snake and a rabbit were racing along a pair of intersecting forest pathways one day, when they collided at the point where the pathways meet.

They immediately began to argue with one another as to who was at fault for the mishap. When the snake remarked that he had been blind since birth, and thus should be given additional leeway, the rabbit said that he, too, had been blind since birth. The two animals then forgot about the collision and began commiserating concerning the problems of being blind. The snake said that his greatest regret was the loss of his identity. He had never been able to see his reflection in water, and for that reason did not know exactly what he looked like, or even what he was. The rabbit declared that he had the same problem. Seeing a way that they could help each other, the rabbit proposed that one feel the other from head to toe, and then try to describe what the other animal was.

The snake agreed, and started by winding himself around the rabbit. After a few moments, he announced, "You've got very soft, fuzzy fur, long ears, big rear feet, and a little fuzzy ball for a tail. I think that you must be a bunny rabbit!" The rabbit was much relieved to find his identity, and proceeded to return the favor to the snake.

After feeling about the snake's body for a few minutes, he asserted, "Well, you're scaly, you're slimy, you've got beady little eyes, you squirm and slither all the time, and you've got a forked tongue. I think you're a lawyer!"

The Rabbit's Thesis

One sunny day a rabbit came out of her hole in the ground to enjoy the fine weather. The day was so nice that she became careless and a fox snuck up behind her and caught her.

"I am going to eat you for lunch!" said the fox.

"Wait!" replied the rabbit. "You should at least wait a few days."

"Oh yeah? Why should I wait?"

"Well, I am just finishing my thesis on 'The Superiority of Rabbits over Foxes and Wolves.'"

"Are you crazy? I should eat you right now! Everybody knows that a fox will always win over a rabbit."

"Not really, not according to my research. If you like, you can come into my hole and read it for yourself. If you are not convinced, you can go ahead and have me for lunch."

"You really are crazy!" But since the fox was curious and had nothing to lose, it went with the rabbit. The fox never came out.

A few days later the rabbit was again taking a break from writing and sure enough, a wolf came out of the bushes and was ready to set upon her.

"Wait!" yelled the rabbit. "You can't eat me right now."

"And why might that be, my furry appetizer?"

"I am almost finished writing my thesis on 'The Superiority of Rabbits over Foxes and Wolves.'"

The wolf laughed so hard that it almost lost its grip on the rabbit.

"Maybe I shouldn't eat you; you really are sick…in the head. You might have something contagious."

"Come and read it for yourself; you can eat me afterward if you disagree with my conclusions." So the wolf went down into the rabbit's hole…and never came out.

The rabbit finished her thesis and was out celebrating in the local lettuce patch. Another rabbit came along and asked, "What's up? You seem very happy."

"Yup, I just finished my thesis."

"Congratulations. What's it about?"

"'The Superiority of Rabbits over Foxes and Wolves.'"

"Are you sure? That doesn't sound right."

"Oh yes. Come and read it for yourself."

So together they went down into the rabbit's hole. As they entered, the friend saw the typical graduate abode, albeit a rather messy one after writing a thesis. The computer with the controversial work was in one corner. And to the right there was a pile of fox bones, on the left a pile of wolf bones. And in the middle was a large, well-fed lion.

The moral of the story:

The title of your thesis doesn't matter.

The subject doesn't matter.

The research doesn't matter.

All that matters is who your advisor is.

The Horse in the Bar

A horse walks into a bar.
The bartender says, "Why the long face?"

The Weasel and the Duck

This weasel and this duck are sitting at a bar. The bartender drops something and goes to pick it up and cracks his back.

The weasel says, "Ya know, I can take care of dat for you. Jus' come into my office and we'll get jou taken care of. Da first visit is only two grand. The second'll cost ya around t'ree grand. The t'ird and final visit weel cost jou a mere five thousand dollars, and jou'll be as good as new. Here's my card."

The weasel gives the bartender his card and hits the road. The bartender looks at the duck and says, "What do you think of that guy?"

The duck says, "Quack."

The Gorilla and the Lion

One day a man in need of a job walks into a zoo to talk to the zookeeper about possibly working there. The zookeeper said no jobs were available but that the man should try the carnival right down the street. As the man started to walk away, the zookeeper noticed the man walked hunched over somewhat and got an idea. So he the stopped the man and said he might have a job for him after all.

"How would you like to be a gorilla?" asked the zookeeper.

"A what?" replied the man.

"A gorilla," answered the zookeeper. "Our gorilla just died and if you put on a gorilla suit, combined with your walk, no one will know the difference. How about it?"

"Okay," said the man, and he went to work.

Well, needless to say, this guy was a natural. Everyone thought he was a real gorilla and enjoyed watching him.

One day, the man noticed a tire hanging on the end of a rope and started swinging on it—the crowds grew. He then noticed a lion's pit next door; he could swing over the lion's pit, swat the lion on the nose, and get back totally untouched. The people loved it and now would come just to see this "gorilla" do his thing.

Well, one day the man swung over the lion's pit, swatted the lion on the nose, and the rope broke!

The lion stared at the man in his gorilla suit and started towards him one step at a time.

The man, seeing this lion coming toward him, started freaking out and began screaming at the top of his lungs, "Help! Help! Help!"

The lion said, "Shut up or we'll *both* lose our jobs!"

The Rabbit from the Laboratory

A rabbit one day managed to break free from the laboratory where he had been born and brought up. As he scurried away from the fencing of the compound, he felt grass under his little feet and saw the dawn breaking for the first time in his life.

"Wow, this is great," he thought. It wasn't long before he came to a hedge and, after squeezing under it, he saw a wonderful sight—lots of other bunny rabbits, all free and nibbling at the lush grass.

"Hey," he called. "I'm a rabbit from the laboratory and I've just escaped. Are you wild rabbits?"

"Yes. Come and join us," they cried.

Our friend hopped over to them and started eating the grass. It tasted so good.

"What else do you wild rabbits do?" he asked.

"Well," one of them said, "you see that field there? It's got carrots growing in it. We dig them up and eat them."

This, he couldn't resist, and he spent the next hour eating the most succulent carrots. They were wonderful.

Later, he asked them again, "What else do you do?"

"You see that field there? It's got lettuce growing in it. We eat it as well."

The lettuce tasted just as good and he returned a while later completely full.

"Is there anything else you guys do?" he asked.

One of the other rabbits came a bit closer to him and spoke softly. "There's one other thing you must try. You see those rabbits there," he said, pointing to the far corner of the field. "They're girls. We shag them. Go and try it."

Well, our friend spent the rest of the morning screwing his little heart out until, completely knackered, he staggered back over to the guys.

"That was fantastic," he panted.

"So are you going to live with us then?" one of them asked.

"I'm sorry. I had a great time, but I can't."

The wild rabbits all stared at him, a bit surprised. "Why? We thought you liked it here."

"I do," our friend replied. "But I must get back to the laboratory. I'm dying for a cigarette."

The Right End of the Dog

A visitor to San Francisco is standing on a street corner waiting for a bus when he notices a blind man and his guide dog. The dog leads the man into the street, where he is brushed by an oncoming car. The man is knocked down, and he rather gingerly gets back up. He calls the guide dog over, reaches into his pocket, pulls out a canine treat, and gives it to the dog.

The visitor, upon seeing all this, walks over to the blind man and says, "That's amazing! Your guide dog led you into a busy street where you were nearly run over by a car, and yet you're giving the dog a treat. You must really love that dog."

The blind man turns to the visitor and says, "No, I'm gonna kick that dog's ass—I'm just trying to find out which end is which."

The Vampire Bat

A vampire bat came flapping in from the night covered in fresh blood and parked himself on the roof of the cave to get some sleep. Pretty soon all the other bats smelled the blood and began hassling him about where he got it.

He told them to go away and let him get some sleep, but they persisted until he finally gave in.

"Okay, follow me," he said and flew out of the cave with hundreds of bats behind him.

Down through a valley they went, across a river and into a forest of trees. Finally he slowed down and all the other bats excitedly milled around him.

"Now, do you see that tree over there?" he asked.

"Yes, Yes, Yes!" the bats all screamed in a frenzy.

"Good!" said the first bat. "Because I didn't!"

When Pigs Fly

SUTTON-ON-TRENT, England, Sept 3 (AFP)—Pigs flew through the air in England Tuesday when a freak tornado crossed a pig farm.

Forty pigs were hurled through the air for over a quarter of a mile as the tornado crashed into a farm at Sutton-on-Trent, near Newark, in central England.

"We looked up and saw these pig-huts swirling around 100 feet (30 meters) up in the air," said witness Allison Reed. "My son shouted that he could see pigs being hurled around in the air among chimney pots and tiles."

Farmer Michael Hewson said many of his animals had died.

The Magic Frog

A man takes the day off from work and decides to go out golfing. He is on the second hole when he notices a frog sitting next to the green. He thinks nothing of it and is about to shoot when he hears, "Ribbit. Nine iron."

The man looks around and doesn't see anyone, so he tries again. "Ribbit. Nine iron." He looks at the frog and decides to prove the frog wrong, puts his other club away, and grabs a nine iron. Boom! he hits a birdie. He is shocked.

He says to the frog, "Wow, that's amazing. You must be a lucky frog, eh?"

The frog replies, "Ribbit, Lucky frog." The man decided to take the frog with him to the next hole.

"What do you think, frog?" the man asks.

"Ribbit, three wood," is the reply.

The guy takes out a three wood and boom! hole in one. The man is befuddled and doesn't know what to say. By the end of the day, the man golfs the best game of golf in his life and asks the frog, "Okay, where to next?"

The frog replies, "Ribbit, Las Vegas."

They go to Las Vegas and the guy says, "Okay, frog, now what?"

The frog says, "Ribbit, roulette."

Upon approaching the roulette table, the man asks, "What do you think I should bet?"

The frog replies, "Ribbit, three thousand dollars, black six."

Now, this is a million-to-one shot that this will win, but after the golf game, the man figures what the heck. Boom! Tons of cash comes sliding back across the table.

The man takes his winnings and buys the best room in the hotel. He sits the frog down and says, "Frog, I don't know how to repay you. You won me all this money and I am forever grateful."

The frog replies, "Ribbit. Kiss me."

He figures why not, since after all the frog did for him, he deserves it. All of a sudden the frog turns into the most gorgeous sixteen-year-old girl in the world.

"And that, your honor, is how the girl ended up in my room."

The Cowboy

There are two church-going women gossiping in front of the country store when a dusty old cowboy rides up. He ties up in front of the saloon, walks around behind his horse, lifts its tail, and kisses the horse full on its asshole.

Repulsed, one of the women asks, "That's disgusting! Why did you do *that?*"

To which the cowboy replies, "I've got chapped lips."

Confused, the woman continues, "Does that make them feel better?"

"No, but it stops me from licking them!"

Who's Got the Boat?

A magician was working on a cruise ship in the Caribbean. The audience would be different each week, so the magician allowed himself to do the same tricks over and over again. There was only one problem: The captain's parrot saw the shows each week and began to understand how the magician did every trick. Once he understood, he started shouting in the middle of the show:

"Look, it's not the same hat!"

"Look, he's hiding the flowers under the table!"

"Hey, why are all the cards the ace of spades?"

The magician was furious but couldn't do anything; it was, after all, the captain's parrot.

One day the ship had an accident and sank. The magician found himself on a piece of wood in the middle of the ocean with the parrot, of course. They stared at each other with hate, but did not utter a word. This went on for a day and another and another.

After a week the parrot said: "Okay, I give up. Where's the boat?"

A Girl and Her Fiancée

A sixty-year-old woman came home one day and heard strange noises in her bedroom. She opened the door and discovered her forty-year-old daughter playing with a vibrator. "What are you doing?" asked the mother.

"Mom, I'm forty years old, and look at me. I'm ugly. I'll never get married so this is pretty much my husband." The mother walked out of the room shaking her head.

The next day, the father came home and heard noises in the bedroom.

Upon entering the room, he found his daughter using the vibrator.

"What the hell are you doing?" he asked.

His daughter replied, "I already told Mom. I'm forty years old now and I'm ugly. I will never get married so this is as close as I'll ever get to a husband." The father walked out of the room shaking his head.

The next day, the mother came home and found her husband with a beer in one hand and the vibrator in the other watching the football game on TV.

"What on earth are you doing?" she cried.

The husband replied, "What does it look like I'm doing? I'm having a beer and watching the football game with my son-in-law!"

A Prison Joke

Two young guys were picked up by the cops for smoking dope and appeared in court on Friday before the judge. The judge said, "You seem like nice young men, and I'd like to give you a second chance rather than jail time. I want you to go out this weekend and try to show others the evils of drug use and get them to give up drugs forever. I'll see you back in court Monday."

Monday, the two guys were in court, and the judge said to the first one, "How did you do over the weekend?"

"Well, your honor, I persuaded seventeen people to give up drugs forever."

"Seventeen people? That's wonderful. What did you tell them?"

"I used a diagram, your honor. I drew two circles like this…"

○   ○

…and told them this (the big circle) is your brain before drugs and this (small circle) is your brain after drugs."

"That's admirable," said the judge. "And you," he said to the second boy, "how did you do?"

"Well, your honor, I persuaded 156 people to give up drugs forever."

"156 people! That's amazing! How did you manage to do that?"

"Well, I used a similar approach." He draws two circles:

"I said (pointing to the small circle) this is your asshole before prison…"

Elevator Fumble

A man walks into a building and gets into the elevator. He presses the button for the fifth floor. At the second floor the most stunning woman he has ever seen gets into the elevator and leans seductively against the wall. The man doesn't know where to look and starts to get very nervous. The woman begins to unbutton her blouse and throws it on the floor. She then takes off her bra and throws it on the floor. At this stage the guy is getting very nervous.

Then she says: "Make a woman out of me!"

He unbuttons his shirt, throws it on the floor, and replies, "Here, iron that."

Not Very Polite

This guy goes into a fancy cocktail lounge and sits down next to a gorgeous woman. After ordering a drink, he turns to her and says, "Pardon me, but can I smell your pussy?"

"Certainly not!" the outraged woman replies.

"Sorry," the guy says. "It must be your feet."

Michael's Baby

Michael Jackson and his wife are in the recovery room with their new baby. The doctor walks in and Michael asks, "Doctor, how long before we can have sex?"

The doctor replies, "I'd wait until he was at least fourteen!"

Another Microsoft Joke

Bill Gates meets Hugh Grant at a Hollywood party. They are talking and Bill says, "I've seen some great pictures of Devine Brown lately, I sure would like to get together with her!"

Hugh replies: "Well, Bill, you know, ever since our incident, her price has skyrocketed. She's charging a small fortune."

Bill (with a chuckle): "Hugh, money's no object to me. What's her number?"

So Hugh gives Bill her number and Bill sets up a date.

They meet and after they finish, Bill is lying there in ecstasy, mumbling, "Devine…Devine…Devine…oh God…now I know why you chose the name Devine."

To which she replies, "Thank you Bill…and now I know how you chose the name…Microsoft."

Apollo

When Apollo Mission Astronaut Neil Armstrong first walked on the moon, he not only gave his famous "One small step for man, one giant leap for mankind" statement but followed it by several remarks, usual com traffic between him, the other astronauts, and Mission Control. Just before he re-entered the lander, however, he made the enigmatic remark "Good luck, Mr. Gorsky."

Many people at NASA thought it was a casual remark concerning some rival Soviet cosmonaut. However, upon checking, there was no Gorsky in either the Russian or American space programs. Over the years many people questioned Armstrong as to what the "Good luck, Mr. Gorsky" statement meant, but Armstrong always just smiled.

Then on July 5, 1995, in Tampa Bay, Florida, while answering questions following a speech, a reporter brought up the twenty-six-year-old question to Armstrong. This time he finally responded. Mr. Gorsky had finally died and so Neil Armstrong felt he could answer the question.

When he was a kid, he was playing baseball with a friend in the back yard. His friend hit a fly ball which landed in the front of his neighbor's bedroom windows. His neighbors were Mr. and Mrs. Gorsky. As he leaned down to pick up the ball, young Armstrong heard Mrs. Gorsky shouting at Mr. Gorsky: "Oral sex! You want oral sex? You'll get oral sex when the kid next door walks on the moon!"

A Halloween Trick or Treat

A young couple was invited to a swanky masked Halloween party. The wife came down with a terrible headache and told her husband to go to the party and have a good time. Being the devoted husband, he protested, but she argued and said she was going to take some aspirin and go to bed. She told him there was no need for him to miss the fun. So he took his costume and away he went.

The wife, after sleeping soundly for one hour, awakened without pain, and as it was still early, she decided to go to the party. Because hubby did not know what her costume was, she thought she would have some kicks watching her husband to see how he acted when she was not around.

She joined the party and soon spotted her husband cavorting around on the dance floor. He was dancing with every nice looking woman he could, and copping a feel here and taking a little kiss there. His wife sidled up to him, and being a rather seductive woman herself, he left his partner high and dry and devoted his time to the new "action."

She let him go as far as he wished; naturally, since he was her husband. Finally he whispered a little proposition in her ear and she agreed, so off they went to one of the cars and had a little bang. Just before unmasking at midnight, she slipped out, went home and put the costume away and got into bed, wondering what kind of explanation he would have for his notorious behavior.

She was sitting up reading when he came in, and she asked him what he had done.

He said, "Oh, the same old thing. You know I never have a good time when you're not there."

Then she asked, "Did you dance much?"

He replied, "I'll tell you, I never even danced one dance. When I got to the party, I met Pete, Bill, and some other guys, so we went into the den and played poker all evening. But I'll tell you…the guy that I loaned my costume to sure had one hell of a time!"

Santa

Santa Claus: What do you want for Christmas, little girl?

Little Girl: I want Barbie and G.I. Joe.

Santa Claus: You mean Barbie and Ken.

Little Girl: No. I mean Barbie and G.I. Joe.

Santa Claus: But Barbie comes with Ken.

Little Girl: No. She only comes with G.I. Joe. She fakes it with Ken.

A Little Friendly Competition

These four gents go out to play golf one sunny morning. One is detained in the clubhouse, and the other three are discussing their children while walking to the first tee.

"My son," says one, "has made quite a name for himself in the home-building industry. He began as a carpenter, but now owns his own design and construction firm. He's so successful in fact, in the last year he was able to give a good friend a brand new home as a gift."

The second man, not to be outdone, tells how his son began his career as a car salesman, but now owns a multi-line dealership. "He's so successful, in fact, in the last six months he gave a friend two brand new cars as a gift."

The third man's son has worked his way up through a stock brokerage. And in the last few weeks has given a good friend a large stock portfolio as a gift.

As the fourth man arrives at the tee box, another tells him that they have been discussing their progeny and asks what line his son is in. "To tell the truth, I'm not very pleased with how my son has turned out," he replies. "For fifteen years, he's been a hairdresser, and I've just recently discovered he's a practicing homosexual. But, on the bright side, he must be good at what he does because his last three boyfriends have given him a brand new house, two cars, and a big pile of stock certificates."

Where Do Babies Come From?

Mother is in the kitchen making supper for her family when her youngest daughter walks in.

Child: Mother, where do babies come from?

Mom: Well dear…a mommy and daddy fall in love and get married. One night they go into their room…they kiss and hug and have sex.

The daughter looks puzzled.

Mom: That means the daddy puts his penis in mommy's vagina. That's how you get a baby, honey.

Child: Oh I see. But the other night when I came into you and daddy's room, you had daddy's penis in your mouth. What do you get when you do that?

Mom: Jewelry, dear.

Triplets

These triplets are in the womb talking about this and that, and presently one triplet says to his brothers, "Listen, if you could have anything you wanted, what would you wish for?"

"I'd wish for a flashlight," the first triplet says. "It's dark in here."

"I'd wish for a raincoat," the second triplet says. "I haven't been dry for I don't know how long."

"How about you?" the first triplet asks the third triplet.

"I'd wish for a shotgun," says the third triplet, "so we could take care of that goddamned gopher who keeps sticking his nose in."

Crazy Kids

A seven-year-old and his four-year-old brother are upstairs in their bedroom. The seven-year-old is explaining that it is high time that the two of them begin swearing. When his little brother responds enthusiastically, the seven-year old says, "When we go downstairs for breakfast this morning, I'll say 'hell' and you say 'ass'." The four-year-old happily agrees.

As the two boys are seating themselves at the breakfast table, their mother walks in and asks her older son what he would like to eat for breakfast. The seven-year-old replies, "Aw, hell, Mom, I'll just have some Cheerios."

WHACK! The surprised mother reacts quickly. The boy runs upstairs, bawling and rubbing his behind. With a sterner note in her voice, the mother then asks the younger son, "And what would *you* like for breakfast?"

"I don't know," the four-year-old blubbers, "but you can bet your ass it's not gonna be Cheerios!"

Train Joke

A mother was working in the kitchen listening to her son playing with his new electric train in the living room. She heard the train stop, and her son said, "All of you sons of bitches who want to get off, get the hell off now, 'cause this is the last stop! And all you sons of bitches who are returning and want to get on, get your asses on the train now, 'cause we're going down the tracks!"

The mother went into the living room and told her son, "We don't use that kind of language in this house. Now go to your room and stay there for *two hours.* When you come out, you may go back and play with your train, but only if you use nice language."

Two hours later, the boy came out of the bedroom and resumed playing with his train. Soon the train stopped and the mother heard her son say "All passengers who are disembarking the train, please remember to take all of your belongings with you. We thank you for riding with us today and hope your trip was a pleasant one. We hope you will ride with us again soon."

She hears the little boy continue, "For those of you just boarding, we ask you to stow all of your hand luggage under your seat. Remember, there is no smoking on the train. We hope you will have a pleasant and relaxing journey with us today."

Then the child added, "And for those of you who are pissed off about the two-hour delay, see the bitch in the kitchen."

Flight Time

A mother and her son were flying Southwest Airlines from Kansas to Chicago. The son (who had been looking out the window) turned to his mother and said, "If big dogs have baby dogs and big cats have baby cats, why don't big planes have baby planes?"

The mother (who couldn't think of an answer) told her son to ask the flight attendant.

So the boy asked the flight attendant, "If big dogs have baby dogs and big cats have baby cats, why don't big planes have baby planes?"

The flight attendant asked, "Did your mother tell you to ask me?"

He said that she had.

So she said, "Tell your mother that it's because Southwest always pulls out on time."

Consummation

This young couple got married. On their honeymoon they were very anxious to consummate the marriage because they were both virgins. They had saved themselves for the right partner and for marriage. Because of their sexual inexperience they were a bit uncomfortable discussing the subject so they came up with the term "doing the laundry" to use in place of "making love" or "having sex." This made them both more comfortable with the whole concept.

Well, the first night of their honeymoon was wonderful. They both had many years of pent up sexual frustration to expend so they "did the laundry" no less than five times that first night and finally fell asleep together completely exhausted.

In the middle of the night the new husband woke up and he was ready to do the laundry again. He gently shook his new wife and asked her, "Can we do the laundry again?" But she was very tired and all of this new abrasive activity had taken its toll on her body. She told him that she just couldn't do it again just yet. Maybe in the morning.

A few hours later the new wife awoke feeling very guilty. Her new husband had saved himself for her for many years. What he had asked for wasn't unreasonable and she decided she should go ahead and "do the laundry with him again." She gently shook him and said, "Honey, I'm sorry I denied you…we can do the laundry again if you want."

He replied, "That's okay—it was a small load. I did it by hand."

Who Do You Marry?

There is a man who has three girlfriends, but he does not know which one to marry. So he decides to give each one five thousand dollars and see how each of them spends it.

The first one goes out and gets a total makeover with the money. She gets new clothes, a new hairdo, manicure, pedicure, the works, and tells the man, "I spent the money so I could look pretty for you because I love you so much."

The second one went out and bought new golf clubs, a CD player, a television, and a stereo and gives them to the man. She says, "I bought these gifts for you with the money because I love you so much."

The third one takes the five thousand dollars and invests it in the stock market, doubles her investment, returns the five thousand dollars to the man and reinvests the rest. She says, "I am investing the rest of the money for our future because I love you so much."

The man thought long and hard about how each of the women spent the money, and decided to marry the one with the biggest breasts.

How Do I Look?

A husband, tired of his wife asking him how she looks, buys her a full length mirror.

This does little to help, as now she just stands in front of the mirror, looking at herself, asking him how she looks.

One day, fresh out of the shower, she is yet again in front of the mirror, now complaining that her breasts are too small.

Uncharacteristically, the husband comes up with a suggestion.

"If you want your breasts to grow, then every day take a piece of toilet paper, and rub it between your breasts for a few seconds."

Willing to try anything, the wife fetches a piece of toilet paper, and stands in front of the mirror, rubbing it between her breasts. "How long will this take?" she asks.

"They'll grow larger over a period of years," he replies.

The wife stops. "Why do you think rubbing a piece of toilet paper between my breasts every day will make my breasts grow over the years?" she asks.

The husband shrugs. "Why not? It worked for your ass, didn't it?"

A Fumble

A group of young businessmen are chatting at the bar, and one of them decides to share his recent embarrassment with the others. He tells them that he was booking a plane ticket to Pittsburgh, but he was so preoccupied with the beautiful breasts of the girl at the counter that instead of saying, "I'd like a ticket to Pittsburgh," he said, "I'd like a picket to Titsburg!"

An older guy nearby hears the story and says, "You know, I had a similar experience with my wife this morning. We were sitting at the breakfast table. and I meant to say, "Darling, could you please pass the butter?" But what came out was, "You bitch, you're ruining my fucking life!"

Wanna Be Fresh

One night, as a couple lies down for bed, the husband gently taps his wife on the shoulder and starts rubbing her arm. The wife turns over and says "I'm sorry honey, I've got a gynecologist appointment tomorrow and I want to stay fresh." The husband, rejected, turns over and tries to sleep.

A few minutes later, he rolls back over and taps his wife again. This time he whispers in her ear, "Do you have a dentist appointment tomorrow too?"

I Want to Be a Fireman When I Grow Up!

A man who worked for a fire company came home from work one day and told his wife, "You know, we have a wonderful system at the fire station. Bell 1 rings and we all put on our jackets. Bell 2 rings and we all slide down the pole. Bell 3 rings and we're ready to go on the trucks. From now on we're going to run this house the same way. When I say 'Bell 1,' I want you to strip naked. When I say 'Bell 2,' I want you to jump in bed, and when I say 'Bell 3,' we're going to screw all night."

The next night he came home from work and yelled, "Bell 1," and his wife took off her clothes. "Bell 2," and his wife jumped into bed. "Bell 3," and they began to screw. After two minutes, his wife yelled "Bell 4."

"What's this Bell 4?" asks her husband.

"More hose," she replied, "You're nowhere near the fire!"

What Soda Is Your Man?

These three women were sitting around one night talking about their boyfriends when they decided they would give their men nicknames based on kinds of soda.

The first woman said, "I'm gonna call Tom 'Mountain Dew,' because he's as strong as a mountain and always wants to do it!"

The second woman said, "I'm gonna call Bruce '7-Up,' because he has seven inches and it's always up!"

The third woman said: "I'm gonna call my man 'Jack Daniels.'"

The other two women responded: "Jack Daniels? But that's a hard liquor."

The third woman replied: "That's my Leroy!"

Anything for Money

Harry and his wife are having hard times, so they decide she'll become a hooker.

She's not sure what to do, so Harry says, "Stand in front of that bar and pick up a guy. Tell him a hundred bucks. If you've got a question, I'll be parked around the corner."

She's not there five minutes when a guy pulls up and says, "How much?"

She says, "A hundred dollars."

He says "Shit. All I've got is thirty."

She says, "Hold on."

She runs back to Harry and says, "What can he get for thirty dollars?"

Harry says, "A hand job."

She runs back and tells the guy all he gets for thirty dollars is a hand job. He says okay, she gets in the car, he unzips his pants, and out pops a huge cock.

She stares at it for a minute, and then says, "I'll be right back."

She runs back around the corner and says, "Harry, can you loan this guy seventy bucks?"

Ethel

Ethel, determined to keep in shape for her husband even if she is in her middle years, is lying on her back on the bed doing her exercises while her husband is removing his contact lenses in the bathroom. Ethel props up her hips with her hands, stretches her legs straight back over her head—and gets her ankles caught in the bed's headframe.

Her husband comes out of the bathroom and squints at her.

"For God's sake, Ethel," he says, "put in your teeth and comb your hair. You're getting to look more like your mother every day."

Anniversary Gift

The Smiths had been happily married for many years and were preparing to celebrate their fiftieth anniversary.

Mr. Smith had always admired his wife's behind. So much so, in fact, that he often referred to her as "beautiful buns."

Mrs. Smith so deeply loved her husband that she decided to have "beautiful buns" tattooed on her bottom for their anniversary.

She went to the tattoo parlor where she stated her desire to Randy, the tattoo artist. Randy said he would be glad to complete this task; however, at three hundred dollars per letter, the cost would be in the range of four thousand dollars (with tip).

Mrs. Smith was aghast and quite upset since the Smiths were not wealthy people and she could not afford this sum. Randy, the ever-helpful tattoo artist, noticed Mrs. Smith's sadness and quickly suggested that she might be able to have the letters "B-B" tattooed, one on each bun, and that her husband would surely realize that these initials signified his endearing name for her ("beautiful buns"). Additionally, having just the two letters to tattoo would put the cost well within Mrs. Smith's budget, $650 (with tip).

On the night of the Smiths' anniversary, Mrs. Smith planned a very seductive candlelight dinner. After eating, Mr. Smith presented his wife with a dozen roses, chocolates, and a diamond anniversary ring. Mrs. Smith was very happy and said, "Wait until you see what I have for you."

At this point she turned around, lifted her skirt, and, bending over, pulled down her panties, revealing her surprise.

Mr. Smith, with a puzzled look, replied, "Who's Bob?"

Cutting Back

"We've got to cut back on household expenses," this rich guy says to his wife. "Do you think I'm made of money? If you could cook, we wouldn't need a chef."

"Chef, hell!" the wife says. "If you could fuck, we wouldn't need a chauffeur."

The Headache

Joe was moderately successful in his career, but as he got older he was increasingly hampered by incredible headaches. When his personal hygiene and love life started to suffer, he sought medical help.

After being referred from one specialist to another, he finally came across a doctor who solved the problem.

"The good news is I can cure your headaches. The bad news is that it will require castration. You have a very rare condition which causes your testicles to press up against the base of your spine. The pressure creates one hell of a headache. The only way to relieve the pressure is to remove the testicles."

Joe was shocked and depressed. He wondered if he had anything to live for. He couldn't concentrate long enough to answer, but decided he had no choice but to go under the knife.

When he left the hospital, his mind was clear, but he felt like he was missing an important part of himself. As he walked down the street, he realized that he felt like a different person. He could make a new beginning and live a new life.

He walked past a men's clothing store and thought, "That's what I need: a new suit." He entered the shop and told the salesman, "I'd like a new suit."

The salesman eyed him briefly and said, "Let's see…size forty-four long."

Joe laughed. "That's right! How did you know?"

"It's my job."

Joe tried on the suit. It fit perfectly. As Joe admired himself in the mirror, the salesman asked, "How about a new shirt?"

Joe thought for a moment and then said, "Sure."

The salesman eyed Joe and said, "Let's see…thirty-four sleeve and…sixteen and a half neck."

Joe was surprised. "That's right! How did you know?"

"It's my job."

Joe tried on the shirt, and it fit perfectly. As Joe adjusted the collar in the mirror, the salesman asked, "How about new shoes?"

Joe was on a roll and said, "Sure."

The salesman eyed Joe's feet and said, "Let's see…nine and a half…wide."

Joe was astonished. "That's right! How did you know?"

"It's my job."

Joe tried on the shoes and they fit perfectly. Joe walked comfortably around the shop and the salesman asked, "How about a new hat?"

Without hesitating, Joe said, "Sure."

The salesman eyed Joe's head and said, "Let's see…7⅝."

Joe was incredulous. "That's right! How did you know?"

"It's my job."

The hat fit perfectly. Joe was feeling great, when the salesman asked, "How about some new underwear?"

Joe thought for a second and said, "Sure."

The salesman stepped back, eyed Joe's waist, and said, "Let's see…size thirty-six."

Joe laughed. "No, I've worn size thirty-four since I was eighteen years old."

The salesman shook his head, "You can't wear a size thirty-four. It would press your testicles up against the base of your spine and give you one hell of a headache."

Is Your Pharmacist Your Friend?

This guy goes to the pharmacist and says, "Listen, these two girls are coming to my place for the weekend and they are hot, very hot. Would you have something to get me going all night? It is going to be a hell of a party."

The pharmacist goes in the back room, comes back with an old dusty bottle, and says, "This stuff is very potent. You drink only one ounce of it and I guarantee that you will be doing the wild thing all night. Let me know about it."

The weekend goes by and on Monday morning, the pharmacist is going to work and at the door of the drug store, the same fellow is there waiting for him. The pharmacist says, "What are you doing here so early? How was your weekend?"

The guy replies, "Quick, open the store, I need Blue Ice!" (Blue Ice is a muscle pain reliever.)

The pharmacist, knowing what the guy had been doing all weekend, says, "Are you crazy? You can't put that on your penis! The skin is way too sensitive."

The guy says, "It's not for my penis, it's for my arm."

Pharmacist says, "What? What happened?"

The guy replies, "Well…I drank the whole bottle of your potion."

"And…?"

"The girls never showed up!"

A Scottish Folk Tale

A Scottish old timer in Scotland is talking to a young man in a bar.

"Lad, look out there to the field," the old man says. "Do ya see that fence? Look how well it's built. I built that fence stone by stone with me own two hands. Piled it for months. But do they call me McGregor the Fence Builder? Nooo."

Then the old man gestured at the bar. "Look here at the bar. Do ya see how smooth and just it is? I planed that surface down by me own achin' back. I carved that wood with my own hard labor for eight days. But do they call me McGregor the Bar Builder? Nooo."

Then the old man points out the window. "Eh, Laddy, look out to sea. Do ya see that pier that stretches out as far as the eye can see? I built that pier with the sweat off me back. I nailed it board by board. But do they call me McGregor the Pier Builder? Nooo."

Then the old man looks around nervously, trying to make sure no one is paying attention.

"But ya fuck *one* goat…"

Oh, Those Irishmen

An Irishman walks into a bar in Dublin, orders three pints of Guinness and sits in the back of the room, drinking a sip out of each one in turn. When he finishes them, he comes back to the bar and orders three more.

The bartender asks him, "You know, a pint goes flat after I draw it. It would taste better if you bought one at a time."

The Irishman replies, "Well, you see, I have two brothers. One is in America, the other in Australia, and I'm here in Dublin. When we all left home, we promised that we'd drink this way to remember the days when we drank together."

The bartender admits that this is a nice custom, and leaves it there. The Irishman becomes a regular in the bar, and always drinks the same way: he orders three pints and drinks them in turn.

One day, he comes in and orders two pints. All the other regulars notice and fall silent.

When he comes back to the bar for the second round, the bartender says, "I don't want to intrude on your grief, but I wanted to offer my condolences on your great loss."

The Irishman looks confused for a moment, then a light dawns in his eye and he laughs.

"Oh, no," he says, "everyone's fine. I've just quit drinking."

Turner Brown

A small white guy goes into an elevator. When he gets in he notices a huge black dude standing next to him. The big black dude looks down upon the small white guy and says, "Seven foot tall, 350 pounds, twenty-inch dick, three pound left ball, three pound right ball, Turner Brown." The small white guy faints!

The big black dude picks up the small white guy and brings him to, slapping his face and shaking him. He asks the small white guy, "What's wrong?"

The small white guy says, "Excuse me, but what did you say?"

The big black dude looks down and says, "Seven foot tall, 350 pounds, twenty-inch dick, three pound left ball, three pound right ball. My name is Turner Brown."

The small white guy says, "Thank God! I thought you said 'Turn around.'"

Cultural Differences

A Frenchman, an Englishman, and a New Yorker are captured by cannibals. The chief comes to them and says, "The bad news is that now that we've caught you, we're going to kill you. We will put you in a pot and cook you, eat you, and then use your skins to build a canoe. The good news is that you get to choose how you die."

The Frenchman says, "I take ze sword." The chief gives him a sword. He says, "Vive la France!" and runs himself through.

The Englishman says, "A pistol for me, please." The chief gives him a pistol. He points it at his head, says, "God save the queen!" and blows his brains out.

The New Yorker says, "Gimme a fork." The chief is puzzled, but he shrugs and gives him a fork. The new Yorker takes the fork and starts jabbing himself all over—the stomach, the sides, the chest, everywhere. There's blood gushing out all over; it's horrible.

The chief is appalled, and asks, "My God almighty, what are you doing?"

The New Yorker says, "So much for your canoe, you stupid fuck!"

Good Ol' Southern Fried Chicken

A woman goes into a restaurant in a small Southern town out in the country. She orders chicken and starts to eat. Eating too fast, she starts to choke on a chicken bone.

Well, these two country boys in the next booth notice she is choking, so they get up and go over to help her. The first country boy drops his overalls and bends over. The second country boy starts licking the first boy's butt. The woman gets completely grossed out and hurls all over the place, dislodging the chicken bone from her throat.

The first boy pulls his overalls back up and says to the other, "You're right Leroy. That hind-lick maneuver works like a charm."

The Missionary

A missionary arrives in darkest Africa and goes to live with a tribe therein. He spends years with the people, teaching them to read and write and the good Christian ways of the white man. One thing he particularly stresses is the evils of sexual sin and "Thou must not commit adultery or fornication!"

One day the wife of one of the tribe's noblemen gives birth to a white child. The people of the village are shocked and demand that the chief talk to the missionary.

"You have taught us the evils of sexual sin, and here is a black woman who gives birth to a white child. You are the only white man that has ever set foot in our village, so it does not take a rocket scientist to figure out what has been going on!"

The missionary replies, "No, no, my good man. You are mistaken. What we have here is a natural occurrence—what is called an albino. If you will look to yonder field you will see a herd of white sheep, and yet among them is one black one. Nature does this on occasion."

The chief pauses for a moment, then says, "Tell you what. You say nothing about the sheep, and I won't say anything about the white child."

The Nuns

Nuns are admitted to Heaven through a special gate and are expected to make one last confession before they become angels. Several nuns are lined up at this gate waiting to be absolved of their last sins before they are made holy.

"And so," says St. Peter, "have you ever had any contact with a penis?"

"Well," says the first nun in line, "I did once just touch the tip of one with the tip of my finger."

"Okay," says St. Peter, "dip your finger in the holy water and pass on into heaven."

The next nun admits that, "Well, yes, I did once get carried away and I, you know, sort of massaged one a bit."

"Okay," says St. Peter, "rinse your hand in the holy water and pass on into heaven."

Suddenly there is some jostling in the line and one of the nuns is trying to cut in front.

"Well, now, what's going on here?" says St. Peter.

"Well, your excellency," says the nun who is trying to improve her position in line, "if I'm going to have to gargle that stuff, I want to do it before Sister Mary Thomas sticks her butt in it!"

A True Confession

Tommy goes into a confessional box and says, "Bless me, Father, for I have sinned; I have been with a loose woman."

The priest says, "Is that you, Tommy?"

"Yes, Father, it is I."

"Who was the woman you were with?" the priest asks.

"I cannot tell you, for I do not wish to sully her reputation."

The priest asks, "Was it Brenda O'Malley?"

"No, Father."

"Was it Fiona MacDonald?"

"No, Father."

"Was it Ann Brown?"

"No, Father, I cannot tell you."

The priest says, "I admire your perseverance, but you must atone for your sins. Your penance will be five Our Fathers and four Hail Marys."

Tommy goes back to his pew. His buddy Sean slides over and asks what happened.

Tommy replies: "I got five Our Fathers, four Hail Marys, and three good leads."

Jagermeister Anyone?

A young man walks up and sits down at the bar.

"What can I get you?" the bartender inquires.

"I want six shots of Jagermeister," responds the young man.

"Six shots? Are you celebrating something?"

"Yeah, my first blow job."

"Well, in that case, let me give you a seventh on the house."

"No offense, sir. But if six shots won't get rid of the taste, nothing will."

Choose Your Seatmate Carefully

A businessman boards a flight and is lucky enough to be seated next to an absolutely gorgeous woman. They exchange brief hellos and he notices she is reading a manual about sexual statistics.

He asks her about it and she replies, "This is a very interesting book about sexual statistics. It identifies that American Indians have the longest average penis and Polish men have the biggest average diameter. By the way, my name is Jill. What's yours?"

He coolly replies, "Tonto Kawalski. Nice to meet you."

Pickle Slicing

Bill worked in a pickle factory. He had been employed there for a number of years when he came home one day to confess to his wife that he had a terrible compulsion. He had an urge to stick his penis into the pickle slicer.

His wife suggested that he should see a sex therapist to talk about it, but Bill indicated that he'd be too embarrassed. He vowed to overcome the compulsion on his own.

One day a few weeks later, Bill came home absolutely ashen. His wife could see at once that something was seriously wrong.

"What's wrong, Bill?" she asked.

"Do you remember that I told you how I had this tremendous urge to put my penis into the pickle slicer?"

"Oh, Bill, you didn't."

"Yes, I did."

"My God, Bill, what happened?"

"I got fired."

"No, Bill. I mean, what happened with the pickle slicer?"

"Oh…she got fired too."

A Sick Old Man

An old man of seventy married a young girl of eighteen. When they got into bed the night after the wedding, he held up three fingers.

"Oh honey," said the young nymph. "Does that mean we're going to do it three times?"

"No," said the old man. "It means you can take your pick."

The Retiring Mailman

It was George the Mailman's last day on the job after thirty-five years of carrying the mail through all kinds of weather to the same neighborhood.

When he arrived at the first house on his route, he was greeted by the whole family there, who roundly and soundly congratulated him and sent him on his way with a tidy gift envelope. At the second house they presented him with a box of fine cigars. The folks at the third house handed him a selection of terrific fishing lures.

At the fourth house, he was met at the door by a strikingly beautiful woman in a revealing negligee. She took him by the hand, gently led him through the door (which she closed behind him), and led him up the stairs to the bedroom where she blew his mind with the most passionate love he had ever experienced.

When he had had enough they went downstairs where she fixed him a giant breakfast: eggs, potatoes, ham, sausage, blueberry waffles, and fresh-squeezed orange juice. When he was truly satisfied, she poured him a cup of steaming coffee. As she was pouring, he noticed a dollar bill sticking out from under the cup's bottom edge. "All this was just too wonderful for words," he said, "but what's the dollar for?"

"Well," she said, "last night, I told my husband that today would be your last day, and that we should do something special for you. I asked him what to give you. He said, `Fuck him. Give him a dollar.' The breakfast was my idea."

The Sex Doctor

A doctor had the reputation of helping couples increase the joy in their sex life, but always promised not to take a case if he felt he could not help them. The Browns came to see the doctor, and he gave them thorough physical exams, psychological exams, and various tests and then concluded, "Yes, I am happy to say that I believe I can help you.

"On your way home from my office, stop at the grocery store and buy some grapes and some doughnuts. Go home, take off your clothes, and you, sir, roll the grapes across the floor until you make a bull's eye in your wife's love canal. Then, on hands and knees, you must crawl to her like a leopard and retrieve the grape using only your tongue.

"Then next, ma'am, you must take the doughnuts and from across the room, toss them at your husband until you make a ringer around his love pole. Then like a lioness, you must crawl to him and consume the doughnut."

The couple went home and their sex life became more and more wonderful. They told their friends, Mr. and Mrs. Green, that they should see the good doctor. The doctor greeted the Greens and said he would not take the case unless he felt that he could help them, so he conducted the physical exams and the same battery of tests. Then he told the Greens the bad news.

"I cannot help you, so I will not take your money. I believe your sex life is as good as it will ever be. I cannot help."

The Greens pleaded with him, and said, "You helped our friends the Browns, now please, please help us."

"Well, all right," the doctor said. "On your way home from the office, stop at the grocery store and buy some apples and a box of Cheerios…"

The Tennis Elbow

Bob complained to his friend, "My elbow really hurts. I guess I should see a doctor."

His friend offered, "Don't do that! There's a computer at the drug store that can diagnose anything, quicker and cheaper than a doctor. Simply put in a sample of your urine and the computer will diagnose your problem and tell you what you can do about it. It only costs ten dollars."

Bob figured he had nothing to lose, so he filled a jar with a urine sample and went to the drug store. Finding the computer, he poured in the sample and deposited the ten dollars. The computer started making some noises and the various lights started flashing. After a brief pause out popped a small slip of paper on which was printed:

> You have tennis elbow.
> Soak your arm in warm water.
> Avoid heavy labor.
> It will be better in two weeks.

Late that evening while thinking how amazing this new technology was and how it would change medical science forever, he began to wonder if this machine could be fooled. He decided to give it a try.

He mixed together some tap water, a stool sample from his dog, and urine samples from his wife and daughter. To top it off, he masturbated into the concoction. He went back to the drug store, located the machine, poured in the sample, and deposited the ten dollars. The machine again made the usual noise and printed out the following analysis:

Your tap water is too hard.
Get a water softener.
Your dog has worms.
Give him vitamins.
Your daughter's on drugs.
Put her in rehab.
Your wife's pregnant.

It ain't yours—get a lawyer.
And if you don't stop jerking off,
your tennis elbow will never get better.

A Scream

How do you make a Jewish girl scream twice?
Fuck her in the ass and then wipe your dick on the curtain.

Little Johnny's Lesson

Little Johnny comes home from school with a note from his teacher, indicating that "Johnny seems to be having some difficulty with the differences between boys and girls," and would his mother, "please sit down and have a talk with Johnny about this."

So Johnny's mother takes him quietly by the hand upstairs to her bedroom and closes the door.

"First, Johnny, I want you to take off my blouse…" So he unbuttons her blouse and takes it off.

"Okay, now take off my skirt…," and he takes off her skirt.

"Now take off my bra…," which he does.

"And now, Johnny, please take off my panties."

And when Johnny finishes removing those, she says, "Johnny, *please* don't wear any of my clothes to school anymore!"

Tickle Me Elmo

Q: What do they give Tickle Me Elmo just before he leaves the factory?
A: Two test tickles.

Just Having a Little Fun with Your Secretary

Mr. Johnson had a new secretary. She was young, had a sweet disposition, and was very polite. One day while taking dictation, she noticed his fly was open. While he was leaving the room, she said, "Mr. Johnson, your barracks door is open."

He didn't understand her remark, but later on he looked down and saw that his zipper was open. He decided to have some fun with his secretary.

Calling her in, he asked, "By the way, Miss Jones, when you saw my barracks door was open this morning, did you also notice a soldier standing at attention?"

The secretary, who was quite witty, replied, "Why, no, sir. All I saw was a little disabled veteran sitting on two duffel bags."

The Tuna Fish Sandwich

A tuna fish sandwich walks into a bar and asks for a beer. The bartender says, "Sorry, we don't serve food in here."

A Trip to Oz

Dan Quayle, Newt Gingrich, and Bill Clinton are traveling in a car together in the Midwest. A tornado comes along and whirls them up into the air and carries them thousands of miles away. When they come down and extract themselves from the vehicle, they realize they're in the land of Oz.

They decide to go to see the Wizard of Oz. Quayle says, "I'm going to ask the Wizard for a brain."

Gingrich says, "I'm going to ask the Wizard for a heart."

Clinton says, "Where's Dorothy?"

To order additional copies of this book,
please send full amount plus $4.00 for
postage and handling for the first book and
50¢ for each additional book.
Send orders to:

Galde Press, Inc.

PO Box 460
Lakeville, Minnesota 55044-0460

Credit card orders call 1–800–777–3454
Phone (612) 891-5991 • Fax (612) 891-6091
Visit our website at http://www.galdepress.com

Write for our free catalog.